Jesus

Jesus

Who was he? What is he like? What has he done for me?

Jesus

Quite Simply, the Greatest

Michael Green

eagle

Guildford, Surrey

British Library Cataloguing in Publication Data. A catalogue record for this book is available from the British Library.

Published by Eagle, an imprint of Inter Publishing Service (IPS) Ltd, P O Box 530, Guildford, Surrey GU2 5FN.

Typset by Eagle Publishing
Printed in Singapore
ISBN No: 0 86347 198 6

Contents

Jesus – The Fact Sheet

Whose name is most frequently used as a swear-word?

Who has a million people and more worshipping him in the UK every week?

Whose name determines the world's calendar and date system?

Jesus Christ

Since little is currently taught about him in school, nothing in adult life, and almost nothing on radio and TV, a few basic facts might well be in order.

- Our primary sources for his life are in four Gospels, written somewhere between A.D. 45 and 80, and based on eyewitness testimony. They are to be found in the New Testament, the second half of the Bible.

- There is further material about him in Jewish and Roman sources of the period.

- Jesus was a Jew, born to a working-class family in Judaea, probably in 7 B.C., but in any case before the death of Herod the Great in 4 B.C. (Later chronology miscalculated the date for the start of our era.)

- On the death of Herod, his kingdom was divided. The northern part, Galilee, was ruled by his son Herod Antipas. The southern part, Judaea, was annexed by Rome and ruled by governors under whom there was much unrest. The most famous of these was Pontius Pilate who governed the province for 10 years, from A.D. 26-36.

- After years in the carpentry business, Jesus set out as a peripatetic teacher and healer (from A.D. 27-30), attracting enormous crowds and provoking the jealousy and opposition of the religious authorities.

- In A.D. 30 (or possibly 33), the Jewish chief priests persuaded Pilate to condemn Jesus to death, as a danger to the peace of the province. The method chosen was crucifixion.

- Three days after his death, Jesus rose again from the grave on the first Easter Day. That event launched the Christian Church, which soon spread worldwide.

- Check it all out for yourself in one of the four Gospels.

Jesus resisted temptation in the harsh hills and ravines of the Judean desert.

8

Jesus

When Napoleon was exiled to the island of St Helena he had plenty of time to think. And this is what he wrote:

> There is something about Jesus Christ I cannot understand. Alexander, Caesar, Charlemagne, and myself have all founded great empires, but on what did these creations of our genius rest? Upon force. But Jesus founded his on love. This very day millions would die for him. I have inspired multitudes with enthusiastic devotion. They would die for me. But to do it, it was necessary that I should be present with the electric influence of my looks, my words, my voice. When I saw men and spoke to them I lit up the flame of devotion in their hearts. But Jesus Christ by some mysterious influence, even through the lapse of eighteen centuries, so draws the hearts of men towards him that thousands at a word would rush through fire and flood for him, not counting their lives dear to themselves.

That is a soldier's assessment. A distinguished Jewish scholar, Claude Montefiore, gives his view like this:

> Jesus is the most important Jew who ever lived. He exercised a greater influence upon mankind and civilization than any other person within the Jewish race or outside it. A Jew whose life and character have been regarded by all the best and wisest people as the greatest religious example of any age.

How about a highly intelligent lawyer and politician, Lord Hailsham?

> The first thing we must learn about him is that we should have been absolutely entranced by his company. Jesus was irresistibly attractive as a man. What they crucified was a young man, vital, full of life and the joy of it, the Lord of life itself, and even more the Lord of laughter, someone so utterly attractive that people followed him for the sheer fun of it. We need to recapture the vision of this glorious and happy man whose mere presence filled his companions with delight. No pale Galilean he, but a veritable Pied Piper of Hamelin who would have the children laughing all round him and squealing with pleasure as he picked them up.

Add to that the fact that more than a third of the entire world profess their allegiance to him two thousand years after his death, and you see how pathetic were the claims of the boxer, Mohammed Ali, that "I am the greatest," or of the Beatles that they were more famous than Jesus Christ.

Jesus taught his disciples on hillsides in Galilee such as this.

Rembrandt was the 17th-century master in conveying a mood and suggesting an atmosphere. Here he depicts the scene in the stable when the shepherds came to worship the new-born Jesus.

What Makes Jesus so Special?

A number of things make Jesus stand out as somebody very special indeed.

Background
He was the eldest child in a two-parent, working-class family from a race that was almost universally disliked in the ancient world. He was born in a hovel in a small town on the edge of the map. He became a refugee in Egypt and managed to return to Judaea some years later to become a carpenter or jobbing builder. He never owned a house. He never went to college. He never wrote a book. He had no social, economic, political, or religious power base. And yet he became the greatest religious leader the world has ever seen, the most influential man in history. We even date our era after him. That makes him rather special.

Influence
His influence is another factor. The whole of subsequent civilization has been influenced by this astonishing carpenter. Medicine, art, literature, humanitarian concerns, liberation, education, owe more to the man of Nazareth than to anyone else throughout history. That makes him a bit special too.

Character

How about his character? I can't get over the fact that nobody has been able to substantiate any charge against his morals in even a single instance. He is the only example we have of the perfect human being: invariably honest, pure, loving, courageous, self-sacrificing, and any other virtue you care to mention. He had them all, and none of the vices. It wasn't like that with Confucius, with Mohammed, with Socrates, or with any of the other great teachers of mankind. That matchless life makes him unique.

Impact

His impact is pretty amazing, too, when you stop to think about it. Whether you go to the aborigines in the center of Australia, or to the Eskimos in Northern Canada, to a Far Eastern land like China (where they reckon there are now some 70 million believers, despite Mao's brainwashing and the persecution), or Argentina, where there is a powerful revival — it is the same story. The biggest influence for good on life and character in all these places is Jesus. have just been among representatives of Prison Fellowship International from 120 countries who are bringing the good news of Jesus to the most hardened criminals in the world, the scum of the prison population, and I have heard story after story of transformed lives as men and

Many artists have been captivated by Jesus's life before he started his public ministry. This late Victorian painting by William Holman Hunt is rich in symbolism as he imagines the carpenter's workshop in Nazareth.

The snow-clad heights of Mount Hermon tower above Galilee.

women have accepted him as their Lord. Indeed, quite a lot of them were at the conference! He has been gone nearly 2000 years. Yet some 70,000 people worldwide entrust their lives to him every day. Don't you think that makes him special?

Teaching

His teaching is another thing that I can't get over. It is so fresh, so revolutionary, so obviously true, so authoritative: he speaks of what he knows. There is nothing tentative about it. Nothing which depends on other writers. He speaks from the Old Testament scriptures and he speaks from God. There are no other sources. And yet the words of this apparently uneducated carpenter have proved the surest guide for all human beings who have tried to follow them. The love for God and for neighbor which he taught are so clearly the best way to go. To live life as God intended, committed to obeying and pleasing him — that is obvious sense. Everything works best when you follow the Maker's instructions. Nobody has ever been able to improve on the teaching of Jesus about God's ideals for living. It is as challenging, powerful, and relevant today as when it left his lips. There aren't many people of whom you could say anything comparable. None, in fact! That marks him out as a bit special.

Miracles

His miracles are simply astounding. They cannot be written off as exaggerations. They are recorded in strand after strand of the Gospel records, and even in hostile Jewish writings like Josephus and the Mishnah. They are never designed to show off. They are never conjuring tricks. They are intended primarily to illustrate who Jesus is and what he has come to achieve. So when he opens the eyes of a blind man, heals a leper, or enables a lifetime cripple to walk, he is not only showing deep compassion, but making a statement about his identity. He is God's messenger to open eyes that are blind to him, cleanse the ghastly mess that disfigures our lives, and rescue us from the moral impotence which keeps all of us cripples.

Some of his miracles affect nature, as when he feeds thousands of people from a few loaves and fish, or walks on water in the midst of a storm. These are functions specially reserved for God Almighty in the Old Testament. It is God who feeds the world and stills the storm. So Jesus is claiming to give a sample of God's own work in controlling the forces of nature and providing sustenance for mankind. Even death is not an impossible obstacle for Jesus. On several occasions he is recorded as raising people from death, notably his friend Lazarus. As he does so he claims, "I am the resurrection and the life. He who believes in me

The mood of the Sea of Galilee can change quickly from calm to storm.

This is how the Dutch master Rembrandt imagined the raising of Lazarus.

will live, even though he dies; and whoever lives and believes in me will never die." Do you see how his claims and his miracles are woven together? They are acts of power, love and healing, to be sure. But that is only half the story. They are acted claims. They are meant to draw our attention to this amazing person, and make us ask if it is reasonable to regard him as just a man, when he can do these things which properly belong to God.

Prophecy

There's another thing that makes Jesus special: his fulfillment of prophecy. The Old Testament scriptures had predicted that a king like David would arise who would have worldwide dominion. A Son of Man would come to God and receive a glorious kingdom which would never be destroyed. A prophet like Moses would give unparalleled teaching to the people of God. There would be a Servant of the Lord whose suffering would be intense and whose death would, in God's mercy, erase the guilt of the people. A Son of God would emerge, whose character would mirror that of God his Father. This coming figure would be born in Bethlehem of David's lineage, but into a very humble family. He would both restore Israel and be a light to the pagans. He would be despised and rejected by the very people he came to rescue from their selfishness. He would die among criminals and his tomb would be supplied by a rich man. But that would not be the end of him. Death would not be able to hold him. He would live again, and God's plans would prosper in his hands. For he would forge a new agreement between God and humankind by means of his self-sacrificial death. Indeed, his death would enable ordinary folk to have the Spirit of God come and take up residence in their lives.

Now these scattered predictions were written hundreds of years before Christ. All of them came true with Jesus. Not some of them: all of them. There is no parallel in the history of the world for prophecies like these, written centuries previously, all coming together in the life of one human being. That human being was Jesus. It makes him very special.

What Does He Claim?

Yes, there are many things that make Jesus special and worthy of our very close attention. But it is his claims which really fascinate me. He claimed that God was uniquely his Father and that he alone had the right to call him "daddy," Abba. Nobody had ever done that. He claimed that he was God's living Bread to feed and nourish us — no less essential than bread is for our bodily well-being. He claimed that he could be like a fountain of water bubbling up in the heart of the believer so that we need never be tortured by that terrible thirst for love and meaning anymore. He claimed that he was the Way to God: he didn't just show the way, he was it. He said he was the Truth about God, not just in his teaching but as a perfect expression of God. He claimed that he was God's very own Life lived out among us human beings. What are we to make of these claims?

There are plenty more, in his own recorded words in the four Gospels. One of the most astonishing is this: "No one knows the Father except the Son and those to whom the Son chooses to reveal him. Come to me, all you who are weary and burdened, and I will give you rest. Take my yoke upon you and learn from me, for I am gentle and humble in heart, and you will find rest for your souls."

The Golden Gate, Old City wall, Jerusalem.

Do you see what he is claiming? That he alone is the way we must follow if we want to discover what God is really like. The good news is that he is more than willing to introduce any of us to his heavenly Father, however much we may have screwed up our lives. The Jews used to say that when you took the yoke of the Old Testament torah upon you, you would discover God. Jesus calmly contradicts this: it is his job to make the introductions! Peace for the soul and rest for the weary follows when we come to him and put our lives in his hands. It is not to be found in a book or a religious system.

It was in this vein that he claimed he was the Light of the world, and that whoever followed him would never walk in darkness. He claimed that he alone of all people had come into the world primarily to die: he would offer up his life as a sacrifice for many — indeed, for all who would accept it. In some mysterious way, his perfect life would atone for ours. Whatever that means, it is a claim nobody else has ever made. And that was not all. He claimed that he would rise again from the carnage of that terrible death by crucifixion: three days later he would show himself alive. What religious teacher has ever made such a claim, let alone substantiated it? It sets Jesus utterly apart. To put him on a level with any other religious leader is not just wrong headed, it is bad taste.

Yes, his claims set him apart from everyone else. They are all the more astounding when you see them against the background of his great simplicity of life, great personal modesty and self-sacrifice. There is nothing bigheaded about Jesus. In his claims he is simply telling us like it is.

So how are we to assess these astounding claims? Are they the meanderings of a madman? Friedrich Nietzsche in the nineteenth century claimed that modern man had killed God and was becoming a superman to fill the gap: but Nietzsche's life had nothing to commend it. He was no superman. He got syphilis and went mad. But Jesus showed no sign of mania alongside his claims. And he who laid such stress on truth can scarcely have set out to deceive his hearers. Had he done so, he would speedily have been shown up, and his teachings would not have had their life-transforming power down the centuries. Very well then, I see no other alternative. He was speaking the truth.

That is the conclusion to which his first followers were driven, though it was the last thing they were predisposed to believe. As loyal Jews they

could not even entertain the possibility that God might become one of them. But as they lived alongside Jesus they could find no other explanation for this amazing man. His friend John spoke for them all when he said, "No one has ever seen God, but God the One and Only who is at the Father's side, has made him known." Can you come up with any other explanation which does justice to the evidence?

On his last evening with his disciples before his arrest, Jesus gave them strict instructions how to remember him through the sharing of his body and blood in the meal Christians celebrate today as Holy Communion.

WHAT IS HIS GOAL?

There is not much doubt about that. It is the subject matter of all the Gospels. Jesus came to bring in the Kingdom of God. Now that may sound a little strange to our ears. If there is a God at all, surely he must be King? True, but humankind has declared independence. We do not want to acknowledge his kingship. We want to do our own thing, and are allergic to anyone giving us guidelines for life, even God. In any case, God is so vague and far away.

Well, Jesus came to show that God is neither vague nor far away. He came to show us in his own life and teaching what God is like. He came to make God near, to bring him into sharp focus. And the burden of his message was that society in general, and each of us in particular, need to turn back to the God we have insulted and rejected. We need to recognize his royal claims over every part of our lives (not some little religious slot). He assures us that when we surrender to him it will not cramp and impoverish our lives, but enrich them with the most profound fulfilment. We will find that going God's way is not a jail sentence; it is what we were made for. And if God is really loving and pure and good and generous, wouldn't it be marvellous to have his will done on earth as it is in heaven? That, at any rate, is what Jesus told us to pray for in the Lord's Prayer. The world would be a very much better place if we prayed and worked for a goal like that.

The Lord's Prayer

Our Father in heaven,

hallowed be your name,

your kingdom come,

your will be done

   on earth as it is in heaven.

Give us today our daily bread.

Forgive us our debts,

   as we have forgiven our debtors.

And lead us not into temptation,

but deliver us from the evil one.

WHAT ARE THE PROBLEMS?

But there are obstacles, massive ones. Jesus encountered them in his own day with the religious opposition of the Pharisees and scribes, the political opposition of the chief priests and the Romans — not to mention the sheer cussedness of men and women in general. There is something very deeply wrong with human nature. When we see the highest, somehow it shames us, and we want to rip it apart and destroy it. That's what they did with Jesus, the best and greatest life that had ever lived. They could not bear to face up to the Light of the world: his rays illuminated their darkness. So they did their best to put the Light out.

Let's have a look at those obstacles to the coming of the Kingdom of God in human society.

1. Wickedness

First there is the whole question of human wickedness. We see it in everyone else: we are often blind to it in ourselves. But Jesus was totally uncompromising on the subject. "What comes out of a man is what makes him 'unclean.' For from within, out of men's hearts, come evil thoughts, sexual immorality, theft, murder, adultery, greed, malice, deceit, lewdness, envy, slander, arrogance and folly. All these evils come from inside and make a man 'unclean.' " Can you argue with that diagnosis by the Great Physician? I can't. I know it is true of me. How about you?

Very well then, if this is the case, we have a problem on our hands. How can a God who is the source of morals, the origin of justice, the fount of goodness — how can such a God have us in his presence when we reek of the opposite? That is what the Bible is getting at when it tells us that we are spiritually dead: we cannot share in the life of this good God. But, amazingly, he loves us. He wants to have us back. But how can he without compromising his standards and pretending that wrongdoing does not matter? If it is God's world, if it is a moral universe, it must matter. And because it matters, God has done something about it.

It would be no good our covering our diseased moral selves with the skimpy garments of religion: they would be see-through. It would be no good our promising God that we would be different in the future: let's face it, we wouldn't. It would be no good protesting how sincere we were: we can be sincere and wrong. No, all our offerings are totally inadequate. That is why God determined to act — to rescue us. What he did was this. He came into our world and lived a perfect life in order to show us what a truly God-centerd human life could be like, and to point the way for our discipleship. Then he allowed that life to be offered up

The love of Jesus was most clearly shown in his death on the cross—possibly the subject most illustrated in world-wide art. Here, 20th-century French artist Rouault powerfully evokes this supreme sacrifice—which provokes the responses of the onlookers.

on a cross in our place.

Not, of course, that we had all deserved crucifixion. But we had all sinned, as the Bible calls it; we had all gone wrong, broken God's laws, and fallen short of his standards. We were, as a result, cut off from God, estranged, alienated, guilty. Call it what you will, there was a great wall between us and God. And God came to us in the person of Jesus and said, in effect, "I love you very much, but evil has to be dealt with. I am going to allow that wall of your misdoings to fall on me and crush me — so that you can have access to God, unrestricted and unashamed." No wonder the Christians sing "Amazing grace, how sweet the sound, that saved a wretch like me." Undreamed-of generosity. A total amnesty by God — what a way to start life in the Kingdom!

2. Moral weakness

But there is a second great obstacle, our moral weakness. Like the scurrilous Roman poet Ovid, we have to admit "I see the better course, and I approve of it — but I follow the worse!" That is not just my weakness and yours; it is universal, and all the greatest thinkers down human history have bewailed it. How can God build a Kingdom with such enfeebled followers? Well, here's how he went about it. He did not stay dead. On the first Easter Day God smashed the shackles of the grave

Sunrise over the Sea of Galilee.

and raised Jesus to a new and endless life. "Raised from the dead, he can die no more. Death can no longer touch him": that was the exultant cry of the New Testament writers. The evidence for his resurrection, by the way, is overwhelming. This is no fairy story happy ending. It is sober truth.

You may say, 'So what?'

The consequences for us are phenomenal. God raised Jesus to his home in heaven and released the spiritual power which had sustained Jesus' life to come and live in ours. Christians call it the Holy Spirit. That was God's brainwave to enable moral cripples to stand upright. He would fill them with his Spirit. There's nothing automatic about it, of course: God wants friends, not robots. It is all too easy for Christians to screw up: we do it all the time. But when we do turn to him and ask for his strength, we find he gives it to us, and gradually a transformation of character takes place which cannot be explained away. We become more and more recognizably Kingdom people.

3. Individualism

The third great obstacle to the coming of the Kingdom was mankind's individualism. It is even more obvious now than it was in Jesus' day: and it is more prevalent in the West than in the rest of the world. Essentially the problem lies in our selfcenterdness and the fragmentation of our society. How was God to deal with that obstacle to Kingdom building? He devised the idea of the church. That is the society of people from every race and background who owe their membership entirely to God's generosity alone. It is not an institution, or a hierarchy, or an establishment, or a building, or an hour a week! It is a community, a family, a counter-culture, of people who may have nothing else in common apart from commitment to the King and to each other. They are determined to live out the Kingdom lifestyle in their relationships and behavior, and to commend the King by word and deed to others. When that really happens, look out. You'll see the Kingdom of God making waves in our society.

Unfortunately, it hasn't always worked out like that.

Why the Opposition?

Lots of people hate Jesus. Remarkable, isn't it, when his life is unquestionably the greatest ever? It does not reflect well on human nature. But then Christians should harbor no illusions about human nature.

1. Persecution

Persecution has accompanied the Christian gospel down the ages. It springs, I think, from this corrupt urge of ours to destroy the best and greatest when we see it. From ancient Rome to modern China or Russia, the followers of Jesus have been relentlessly persecuted. It is more subtle, but just as prevalent, in the sustained opposition of the West to the way of Jesus and its marginalization of his followers. The fear is that Jesus will prove a threat to worldly power as exercised by those doing the persecuting. Well, there is something in that. But the Kingdom of God is not about earthly power and glory. It is about contending for justice and peace, and caring in love and self-giving for those whom modern power structures oppress. Not surprisingly, those people in power are not best pleased by this gentle revolution.

This early 5th-century mosaic from Ravenna, Italy, shows Jesus as shepherd, sitting in judgement and separating with great compassion the sheep from the goats. It is one of the earliest representations of Jesus.

2. Skepticism

Skepticism is another response to Jesus which has been there from the start. Nowadays it generally shows in civilized disdain, or in the passionate intellectual opposition to Christianity which you find in that evolutionary crusader Richard Dawkins. One of the most interesting assaults on Christianity I have come across is Bertrand Russell's *Why I am not a Christian*. Lord Russell was one of the sharpest philosophers this century has produced, and yet his assault on Christianity is pathetically thin. He simply does not begin to come to terms with the person of Jesus, his character, death, resurrection, and pervasive attractiveness. There is much in historic Christianity for skeptics to deride and expose: but they cannot do that with Jesus. Perhaps that is why most of them don't try. They direct their artillery on the Christian church and its record.

3. Christianity as state religion

Christendom is a somewhat surprising but nonetheless real enemy of the authentic Jesus. After 250 years of opposition, often of outright persecution, the Roman Empire succumbed to Jesus Christ, and in A.D. 313 the Emperor Constantine declared Christianity to be the religion of the Empire. A new era of cooperation between church and state began. It lasted for more than a thousand years, and the remnants are with us today, especially in the state churches on the Continent, the English Establishment and American civil religion. When that codependency between church and state occurs, the church is no longer salt and light in society. It gets severed from its missionary purpose. It becomes compromised by its dependence on state recognition and patronage. If it is to reflect the love and power, the challenge and integrity of Jesus, the church has to turn its back on its idolization of worldly systems of power and thought. The theologian Richard Niebuhr recognized that too often today we have an enfeebled church "which is in retreat and which has made compromises with the enemy in thought, in organization and in discipline." Such a religion is miles from the teaching of Jesus.

4. Religion
Religion is another deadly foe of Jesus Christ. It was the religious people who were so infuriated by his compassion for the ignorant and the poor whom they despised, so angry that he gave little consideration to the temple services and the ecclesiastical rule book, so scandalized by his determination to be impressed by the state of the heart not the extent of the ceremonial, that they hounded him to the cross. Real Christianity is not, strictly speaking, a religion at all. It is the foe of religion.

Religion is indeed, as Bernard Shaw proclaimed, a beggar's refuge. It represents our attempt to climb up to God by means of our worship, our intelligence, our good deeds and the like. Christianity is not a *religion* at all. It is a *rescue* — which is why so many respectable people, proud of their own fancied goodness, fight shy of it. It is a rescue and it is a *relationship*. A relationship day by day with the living Jesus, which is a launchpad to getting involved, with other believers, in the needs of real people, and of becoming a godly influence in today's society.

We are all well aware today, in this global village, of the tremendous harm done by religion, whether in Serbia, Ireland, Kashmir, or Nigeria. It is one of the most powerful and most destructive forces in the world.

WHAT IS GOD'S KINGDOM?

But the Kingdom of God is not like that. It can never be identified with culture, though it operates in all cultures. It can never be identified with a building or an institution, though it may make use of them. It can never be identified with a denomination: it transcends them all. It is nothing to do with an hour on Sunday, but everything to do with the totality of daily, secular life in which God's ambassadors are trying to embody his kingly rule.

This is the Christianity which is growing apace in the two-thirds World. This is the Christianity which is resolutely following Jesus and his way of life, cost what it may. This is the Christianity which cares passionately about the poor, the abused, the criminals, the institutional evils in our world, and throws itself into fighting them. This is the Christianity which has nothing to do with political correctness and the suave chaplaincy to a corrupt society. It is bold, fearless, totally committed to loving God and neighbor, and to drawing others to the Lord who first of all fills us with his love and then makes it glow out to others. It is all about God's freedom fighters in his Kingdom.

There are all sorts of imitations of this marvelous vision, this passionate counter culture.

Some want the *King without the Kingdom*. They are concerned with individual salvation and personal ethics but have no vision for reaching society at large. Theirs is a privatised faith, with little commitment to corporate impact on the structures of our world.

Others want the *Kingdom without the King*. They are deeply involved in issues of social and political concern. Justice, housing conditions, the destruction of racism — all these admirable things are high on their agenda. But there is no surrender to Jesus, no living friendship with him at the heart of all this activity. It is a man-centered program, as if we human beings could bring the Kingdom in. We can't. It is God's Kingdom, and only he can do it.

A third category think that *the church is the Kingdom*. God forbid! How terrible it would be if the Kingdom of God turned out to be no more than the corrupt, feeble, introspective church which is often all that the nation sees. God's Kingdom includes the church, but is far bigger. God is King in his world, even though that kingship is often veiled. One day that veil will be ripped aside, and we shall see King Jesus returning in triumph to the world for which he has died. That is the New Testament hope for the climax of all history. It could come sooner than we imagine.

How Can I Join Up?

We have seen a little of what Jesus is like: his person, his claims, his achievement, and his objectives for human society. We have seen some of the opposition and misunderstandings which have kept many people from him. But now he says to us, as he said to the disciples long ago, "Come, follow me."

It is not difficult to begin Christian discipleship. But it is very challenging. At its simplest, it involves something like this.

Recognize

First, I must recognize that God has a purpose for this broken world, which will reveal more and more of what his Kingdom is like. He wants to see harmony for discord, peace for war, justice for oppression, virtue for vice, love for hate. And I must be willing to allow God's Kingdom to come in my life before I try to bring it about elsewhere. Simple enough, but very humbling.

Ask

Second, I must ask God to clean me up. The seeds of the troubles in the world are all to be found in me. Not all those seeds have germinated, thank goodness, but lots of them have, and I need a radical springcleaning. He has, mercifully, provided for precisely that by his death on the cross. He is alive and able to come and attend to it personally, once I put myself at his disposal.

Determine
Third, I must determine that this is to be no passing decision, no recovery of the "feel good factor," no turning over of a new leaf. It is nothing less than revolution. It will affect my finances, my prayers, my lusts, my home life, my interests, my companionships, my whole direction in life once I start to become a disciple, a learner in the Jesus School. If I allow God's Kingdom to be born in me, it will be costly but infinitely worthwhile.

Open up
Fourth, I must open up to the King. The King of glory became the suffering servant of sinful humanity when he died for us on the cross. He is now risen, alive, and only too willing to start the needed transformation within our lives. But we have to let him do it. He will not force his way in.

Look at this picture of Holman Hunt's *The Light of the World* overleaf. You may or may not like the Pre-Raphaelites. That is not the point. The point is encapsulated in the words of Jesus which inspired this painting:

"Here I am! I stand at the door and knock. If

anyone hears my voice and opens the door, I will come in and eat with him and he with me."

You'll find those marvellous words in the last book of the Bible, chapter 3 verse 20. They mean a lot to me. They led me into the Kingdom!

Do you get the imagery? Our lives are like that house: dark, isolated, with weeds growing up the door. Jesus is the Light of the world. He could be our Light, too. He stands patiently and waits until we decide to invite him in. His hands are scarred by the marks of the nails. His eyes are full of patient love. His dress symbolises his purity (white) and self-sacrifice (red). He is crowned with thorns: the crucified and risen King is here in person. He has every right to enter that house. After all, he constructed it in the first place. And when we, the tenants, decided to steal it from him, he bought it back at incredible cost on the cross. It is rightly his: indeed *doubly* his. He made it. He bought it. But he will not come in until and unless the tenant asks him.

You are the tenant.

The Light of the World, by William Holman Hunt.

What he longs for you to do is to say something like this:

Jesus, I want you to be my King.

I want to be part of your Kingdom on this needy earth. I know I can't do it on my own.

So I ask you to come into my life. Put your unseen but powerful Spirit into my inner being. Clean me through and through.

You have promised, "If anyone opens the door, I will come in." Well, here and now I open the door as best I know how. Please come in and never leave me.

And I pledge to you that I will get involved in the work of your Kingdom until my dying day.

The words aren't important. The sentiment is. And when you have done it, go, tell someone else — in the first instance, someone who would understand! Then get stuck in with God's freedom fighters, believers who are genuinely Kingdom people, and *really let it show*!

That's how the Kingdom spreads.